Poems in
the Porch

Poems in the Porch

The Radio Poems of John Betjeman

Edited by
Kevin J. Gardner

continuum

Continuum UK
The Tower Building
11 York Road
London SE1 7NX

Continuum USA
80 Maiden Lane
Suite 704
New York
NY 10038

www.continuumbooks.com

This collection first published 2008
Reprinted 2008

British Library Cataloguing-in-Publication Data
A catalogue record for this book is available from the British Library.

ISBN 9781847063281

Designed and typeset by Benn Linfield
Printed and bound by MPG Books, Cornwall

'But if it is not true, why was I born? And if it is true, nothing else is of so much importance.'

John Betjeman

CHRISTMAS DAY, 1947
BBC RADIO

TABLE OF CONTENTS

PREFACE

This volume is an attempt to reconstruct a complete edition of John Betjeman's 'Poems in the Porch', those poems that Betjeman wrote for, and read on, BBC radio between 1953 and 1957. All research on Betjeman must acknowledge the groundbreaking work of three devotees of the late poet and broadcaster. Scholars of Betjeman must begin with Bevis Hillier's magisterial three-volume biographical trilogy: there, especially in the middle volume, Hillier amply recounts the triumphs and failures of Betjeman's career in broadcasting.[1] Following this project, in an impressive recovery of Betjeman's radio broadcasts previously hidden in archives and published now in three volumes, Stephen Games has provided a substantial record of Betjeman's radio career, laying out for our consumption a marvellous feast of broadcast journalism.[2] It is the pioneering work of the bibliographer William Peterson, however, that truly makes this edition possible. All future scholars owe a debt of gratitude to Peterson's many years of archival research, slogging through and cataloguing the massive collections of Betjeman papers across the UK and North America.[3] Peterson, Games and Hillier have each in their distinct ways been trailblazers in our understanding of the life of Betjeman, and the importance of their unique contributions should not be underestimated. What we now know of Betjeman's radio career in particular, then, we owe to these three scholars.

The story of Betjeman's radio poems, his 'Poems in the Porch', has not yet been told, however, and the extent of this series of poems is not widely known. A few of the poems in this volume may be familiar to readers today, yet many of them will not be known to readers at all, since most of them are not published in Betjeman's COLLECTED POEMS. Of the 18 poems Betjeman is known for certain to have read in the 'Poems in the Porch' series, only 11 have ever been published; and of these 11, only six are in the COLLECTED POEMS, some quite altered from their original broadcast states. The rest have not appeared anywhere in print before. For some of those published here for the first time, Betjeman did not supply a title. I have taken the rather extreme liberty of doing so, and I hope that I have done so in the spirit of the author himself. The resulting volume contains the 18 known poems Betjeman read on air, two others that he might have read, and two unfinished manuscripts that were likely intended as future broadcast poems.

For the kindness and assistance of so many people in helping me see this book to print I have a long list of thanks and acknowledgement. Foremost I must acknowledge the generosity of the family and estate of the late Sir John Betjeman in authorizing the publication of this edition, and to Tom Williams of Aitken Alexander who represented the estate. For providing the manuscripts of unpublished poems, letters and broadcast scripts, I am indebted to the

University of Victoria's McPherson Library Special Collections, the BBC's Written Archives Centre and the British Library. In particular, I would like to acknowledge Danielle Russell and Terry Tuey at Victoria and Louise North at the WAC for their patience with my numerous requests and their willingness to aid my research. Thanks is due to Rosemary Irvine, who graciously responded to my queries about Betjeman's collaboration on one poem with her brother, the Revd Prebendary Gerard Irvine and to Roger Pringle, who generously shared copies of manuscripts from his personal Betjeman collection, I remain profoundly indebted.

I am also grateful for the assistance of many people at Baylor University, where it is my great good fortune to teach English literature. Among these are Truell Hyde, Vice Provost for Research, and Jan Nimmo, Assistant Vice Provost for Research, and the staff of the Office of Sponsored Programs, who awarded me an Arts and Humanities Faculty Development Grant for this project. I would also like to thank Ken Carriveau in Baylor's Moody Memorial Library for helping me to begin the process of contacting libraries and archives abroad about accessing Betjeman's manuscripts, and I am always grateful to my colleagues in the Department of English for their encouragement of my research.

I am deeply appreciative of the many wonderful people at Continuum for seeing this project through to publication. I am especially grateful to my editor, Ben Hayes, for his patience in guiding my proposal through the many hurdles between manuscript and publication, and to Robin Baird-Smith, publishing director at Continuum, for his particular support of my work on Betjeman.

I would also like to acknowledge my fellow Betjephiles, who paved the way for this project with their groundbreaking research. In particular, it has been an incredible honor to receive the encouragement of Bevis Hillier, Stephen Games, Bill Peterson, Roger Pringle and Anthony Thwaite. I trust that this volume merits the generous support they have shown to me, and to them I will always be indebted.

Finally, it is the greatest fortune in life to be blessed with a loving family. The completion of this project I attribute to the support and confidence placed in me by my wife, Hilary, and son, Graham. For their love and encouragement I am eternally thankful, and to them I dedicate this volume.

Kevin J. Gardner

Waco, Texas, November 2007

---

1 See JOHN BETJEMAN: NEW FAME, NEW LOVE (London: John Murray, 2002), chapters 10, 21 and 29.

2 See also Games's 'Introduction' to his first collection, TRAINS AND BUTTERED TOAST: SELECTED RADIO TALKS (London: John Murray, 2006), pp. 1–29.

3 JOHN BETJEMAN: A BIBLIOGRAPHY (Oxford: Clarendon Press, 2006).

INTRODUCTION

One early autumn evening, now more than 50 years ago, a resonant voice crackled across the airwaves of the BBC, performing the lines of an Anglican church mouse.

> Here among long-discarded cassocks,
> Damp stools, and half-split-open hassocks,
> Here where the Vicar never looks
> I nibble through old service books.
> Lean and alone I spend my days
> Behind this Church of England baize.

Lonely, devout and just a tad hypocritical, the little mouse clings to a church in decline while turning up his wee nose at the rodents who attend only on special occasions. The poem, of course, was John Betjeman's 'Diary of a Church Mouse'. With its unique blend of whimsy and pathos, and a genial touch of satirical wit, all encased in a perfection of metre and rhyme, it was an immediate delight for those fortunate enough to be listening to the BBC's West of England Home Service on the evening of 6 October 1953.

And so began a remarkable and little known chapter in the life of one of the great icons of twentieth-century England. In 1953, John Betjeman was a moderately successful man of letters – a poet who had published four original volumes of verse, a critic and reviewer with a large body of somewhat ephemeral journalism and a number of books on English architecture and topography, and an occasional broadcaster with a growing following. That year he commenced a series of poems about life in the Church of England that he wrote intentionally for reading on the wireless. It would launch him on a path to fame that would help him to become the bestselling poet of the twentieth century.

Having worked in broadcasting for 20 years, Betjeman's experience on BBC radio was substantial. Following the war, his popularity and reputation were such that he could use the airwaves to express quite personal views. It was thus in the late 1940s that listeners of the BBC became aware of Betjeman's interest in religion. Starting with stories about church crawling, Betjeman gradually made the transition from talks about ecclesiastical architecture into more overtly religious discussions. For instance, in 1947 Betjeman's talk on 'Christmas Nostalgia' began with an unfolding of childhood memories, but evolved into an affirmation of the religious truths underpinning the secular celebrations of gift giving.

Contemplating the splendour of creation, Betjeman concluded, 'I cannot believe that I am surrounded by a purposeless accident. But can I believe this most fantastic story of all: that the Maker of the stars and of the centipedes became a baby in Bethlehem not so long ago.' It is a simple enough matter to accept the idea of a rational creator, but the doctrine of the Incarnation poses greater difficulties in belief. While there is little doubt that

Betjeman suffered doubts, on this day he set them aside. 'Beyond my reason, beyond my emotions, beyond my intellect I know that this peculiar story is true.' Betjeman's belief here does not seem daubed on for the effect of a radio performance. He reiterates his assurance with rhetorical force, concluding with the profound yet simple effect of hearing 'Once in Royal David's City' sung in the chapel of King's College, Cambridge. 'And as I heard it I knew once more – knew despite myself – that this story was the Truth.'[1]

Clearly, Betjeman held strong opinions about religion, spiritual questions never being far from his mind. His natural instinct was to doubt, yet he makes clear that divine grace could overwhelm that doubt with certain belief. Bevis Hillier notes that Betjeman's 'attitude is traditional Christian orthodoxy: mankind is fallen and sin is the lasting result'.[2] He had no qualms about using the radio to air his beliefs, a practice that probably struck some listeners as proselytizing. But it was to atone for his certainty of sin that Betjeman felt compelled to share his faith. As Stephen Games writes, 'Religious broadcasts became his acts of grace.'[3]

At the same time that Betjeman was discovering his popularity as a BBC broadcaster, he was increasing in stature and fame as a poet, each half of his career bolstering the other. The first 'collected' edition of his verse appeared in 1948; this volume was SELECTED POEMS and was edited by John Sparrow, fellow (and future warden) of All Souls College, Oxford, and a friend of Betjeman as well as an adviser to him on literary matters. Following the triumph of this publication, Betjeman was asked to read a selection of poetry on the BBC's Third Programme, broadcast on 20 August 1949. Betjeman had a natural style of delivery, self-deprecating and humble, weaving light and personal commentary into the reading of his poems to make the verse more accessible.

Owing to the popularity of this programme, Betjeman agreed to a second such broadcast. Among the poems he read on 6 October 1949 was an early draft, only two stanzas long, of 'Sunday Morning, King's Cambridge', a poem he had begun in 1947 but did not complete and publish until 1954. Describing the difficulty of writing the poem, Betjeman confessed that he was unsatisfied with the final stanza and would read only the first two. 'I don't know whether they are much good', he wrote, 'but King's Chapel really is such a blaze of glory and beauty, especially inside, that I've always wanted to get it into verse.' After reading two stanzas, interspersed with more commentary, Betjeman concluded with an exquisite appreciation of the beauty of the chapel at King's in the full glory of its choir and organ. 'It's absolutely that one experience, I think, that England has got above any country in the world, in the way of architecture and music welded together.'[4]

Thus Betjeman was to some degree already established as a poet of the airwaves when the Revd Martin Willson, director of religious programming at the BBC's West region offices in Bristol, approached Betjeman about creating some original poems designed specially for the radio. Betjeman eagerly embraced the unique concept. Beginning in 1953, and over the course of more than three years, Betjeman read a series of poems on a programme called 'The Faith in the West'. This programme, for which he was already supplying occasional talks about his visits to remote churches and about such topics as 'The Victorian Sunday', was a weekly religious broadcast on the BBC's West of England Home Service. (Betjeman was a regular contributor to this programme from 1951 to 1957.)

The poems, known collectively as 'Poems in the Porch', established the pleasing fiction – though Betjeman was of course known to be the author – that they were the anonymous contributions posted on the notice board in the porch of the church of Stoke St Petroc by one of its parishioners. (In his COLLINS GUIDE TO ENGLISH PARISH CHURCHES, Betjeman described two churches dedicated to St Petroc in Cornwall, but this one is strictly fictional.) Betjeman was quite keen on the project, at least initially. At first, the radio poems came easily and quickly, as Betjeman produced a new poem at the rate of one a month, with 'Diary of a Church Mouse' introducing the series, that gently satirical exploration of Christian hypocrisy, followed by 'Electric Light and Heating', a verse rendering of Betjeman's irritations over the modernization of ancient churches.

Soon, however, the pressure to produce an original poem every month began to mount. Facing many deadlines, Betjeman succumbed to holiday pressures in December of 1953 and read an older poem. 'Christmas' had been published in HARPER'S BAZAAR in 1947, but as it did not appear in a collection of his poetry until A FEW

LATE CHRYSANTHEMUMS was published in 1954, this was the first introduction for much of the public to what would soon become a beloved seasonal classic. Few people now realize that this poem, so often recited at school and church pageants, was in fact the third of Betjeman's 'Poems in the Porch'.

'The Faith in the West', the programme in which Betjeman read these poems, ran on Tuesdays from 7.00 to 7.30 pm and comprised several regular features in addition to the poems. For at least the first few broadcasts, the structure of the programme remained the same. The first segment was 'Prayer in a Busy Life', a sort of practical instruction in prayer, presented by Norman Elliott. This was followed by a 'Poem in the Porch' – sometimes read live and sometimes recorded in advance. The final two segments were 'Music for Worship', introduced by Graham Hooper, and a concluding segment with a rotation of guest presenters whose topics might range from devotionals to book reviews to chapters in Christian history. The whole programme was presented by Martin Willson.

At the first programme, Willson, introducing Betjeman as initiating a new feature on the programme, created the perception that each poem would be read from the church mouse's diary. Following Betjeman's reading, Willson stated that 'the mouse had a distinct sting in its tail, I thought. Another unusual thing about him. We don't know yet much about the Church he lives in – perhaps we'll hear more later.' Willson then attempted to segue from Betjeman's humorous poem to the more serious segment to follow. 'But he [the mouse] must know the Church Service very well indeed, even if the singing isn't very good. It's not very good in a lot of churches', Willson went on, moving not so gracefully into Hooper's segment on how liturgical responses ought to be sung.[5]

The fiction of the poems' being posted in the porch of the church of St Petroc was not established until the second broadcast. 'Now, many of you will remember the page we had a month ago from the Diary of a Church Mouse. We hoped to have another page for you today, but to tell you the truth I'm not quite sure whether what we have for you is part of this Diary or not.' Injecting his own brand of humour, Willson continued with his introduction. 'There's a suspicion that the mouse got so hungry after the Harvest decorations had all been removed that he may have devoured the Diary. But we have found a poem on the noticeboard in the Porch – the Church in question, by the way, is that of Stoke St Petroc, and John Betjeman is here to read it to you.'[6]

It quickly became clear that the idea of anonymous poems posted in the porch was a framing device that would work better than the device of a devout rodent's diary. Church mice probably did not care quite as much about the aesthetic atrocities of electrical lighting dilemmas as Martin Willson did, who confessed in the second pro-gramme to 'a great deal of sympathy with [Betjeman's] point of view. In fact,' Willson avowed, 'I'd go back to can-dles rather than on to electric light.'[7] By the third pro-gramme the framing device was firmly in place. 'And now we move on to some more Poetry in the Porch, the fictional Porch of the Church of Stoke St Petroc, somewhere in the West Country,' intoned Willson. 'And all I'll say about this one is lucky parishioners to [SIC] have their faith proclaimed to them in such a telling and attractive manner. And here is John Betjeman coming into the porch to read out the poem for us.'[8]

Throughout the early months of 1954, Betjeman continued the pattern of reading one new poem per month on 'The Faith in the West'. These poems were 'Blame the Vicar', 'Septuagesima', 'Churchyards' and 'The Friends of the Cathedral'. Following the first seven poems, Betjeman took a hiatus. It was in the spring of this year that Betjeman was approached by the SPCK with a request to publish the radio poems. Betjeman was no doubt surprised to discover the popularity of his verses. Though he had received numerous requests for permission to reprint poems, especially from parishes wanting to include particular verses in their magazines and newsletters, the idea of publishing a permanent volume of poems that had been written for reading aloud was a different matter.

Still, the Revd F. N. Davey, Editorial Secretary in the publication offices of the SPCK, prevailed upon Betjeman, who eagerly embraced the project after persuading his friend, John Piper, to illustrate the poems. The slim volume, with seven drawings rendered in blue ink, was published on 8 October 1954, one year after the 'Poems in the Porch' series had commenced. Piper's illustrations included headstones, a vicarage lawn, church interiors – a simple nave and chancel, a little vestry, and a tangle of wires and ducts defacing a medieval church wall. The volume contained only six of the original seven poems; 'Christmas' had already been published in A FEW LATE CHRYSANTHEMUMS that year, and so was excluded for copyright reasons.

Betjeman's poems were anything but a theological challenge; perhaps one of the reasons accounting for the public's appreciation of the poems was their orthodoxy. The SPCK quibbled, however, over one phrase of Betjeman's in the poem 'Churchyards'. In his broadcast, Betjeman had used the phrase 'When Jesus, whom men thought had died', but Fr Davey raised a theological objection on the basis that Jesus had really died, suggesting in its place 'Men thought was dead'. Betjeman was happy to comply, but desiring to preserve the rhyme offered the more metrically apposite 'When Jesus who indeed had died'. Everyone seemed happy with the emendation, which survives in all subsequent publications of the poem.

Betjeman was nervous about the reception. He had, of course, written the poems specifically to be heard by listeners, not pondered over by readers, and so they are simpler, lighter pieces than much of his other verse. Betjeman thus encouraged the placement of John Piper's name above his own on the cover and title page, and insisted that the following note be included: 'These verses do not pretend to be poetry. They were written for speaking on the wireless, and went out over the Western Region at the request of the Reverend Martin Willson, Director of Religious Broadcasting in the West. Owing to numerous requests for copies of them, the SPCK has kindly consented to publish them in printed form, and in order to compensate for the short-comings of the verse, I have prevailed upon my friend, Mr John Piper, to provide the illustrations.'[9]

The public did not share Betjeman's anxiety about the quality of the verse. To his tremendous surprise, the initial press run of 5,000 copies sold out within a month, and it was followed by another eight impressions released over the ensuing ten years. By June of 1955, nearly 15,000 copies had been sold, and Betjeman had earned royalties of over £75.[10] (This was not a large sum at all; its purchasing power in 2006 pounds is roughly £1,400.)

In November of 1954, a month after publication of POEMS IN THE PORCH, Betjeman returned to the airwaves with more original poems, reading five poems over the six-month period from November 1954 to April 1955. Betjeman was beginning to find the composition of the poems difficult. Poetic inspiration was surely hard to com-mand on schedule, and thus he began to make excuses. Though Betjeman felt he had exhausted the possibilities, the public's appreciation did not wane, and their requests for more were unrelenting. Thus Martin Willson kept after him, and following another hiatus of five months, Betjeman returned in October 1955, reading four (or perhaps five) more poems over a six-month period. Yet another hiatus of six months was followed by two (or perhaps three) final poems, the last one airing on 1 February 1957.

In the summer of 1955, Betjeman had initiated talks with Fr Davey at the SPCK about a second volume of poems that would contain all the subsequent poems Betjeman had read since POEMS IN THE PORCH had been published. In a letter of 1 June 1955, largely complaining about confusions over royalties, Betjeman mentioned that 'There are, incidentally, five new verses which were done during the last session of Faith in the West and which you might like to publish as a new pamphlet, to be called "Verses in the Vestry".' Davey responded with interest on 3 June, as the first volume 'has done well enough for a sequel to be most desirable.' By July, Davey had decided that it would be best to postpone the volume until the following year as it was too late to get it out as a Christmas book in 1955.[11]

Betjeman and the SPCK were eager to proceed with VERSES IN THE VESTRY, and Betjeman was glad for the delay as more radio poems were forthcoming that would enlarge the new volume. Unfortunately, a series of snags prevented the book from ever being published. The first difficulty involved the illustrations. Most of the later poems were about people, and Piper was much more comfortable illustrating buildings. Betjeman tried to recruit his friend Osbert Lancaster, who was an exceptional caricaturist, but Lancaster was too busy to take on the project. Moreover, Jock Murray, Betjeman's primary publisher, had begun to nose into the publication and had objected to Lancaster's involvement.

A second and more troublesome problem appeared when Murray, who had heretofore published all of Betjeman's books of verse except his first (MOUNT ZION had been published by Edward James in 1931), suddenly took interest. Thinking the poems too ephemeral or the pamphlet format too insignificant, Betjeman had never offered POEMS IN THE PORCH to Murray, who according to Betjeman was mildly hurt over the perceived snub. In any case, the great success of that volume awakened Murray's business sense, and he began to press for a joint imprint, arguing that his firm could take the volume into markets that the SPCK could not reach. Davey was sceptical, knowing that Murray's interest was only based on the SPCK's financial success with POEMS IN THE PORCH. 'We do not want to be the dog in the manger,' wrote Fr Davey, 'but . . . as we had to take the initial risk . . . it would be unreasonable of us to share the profits of VERSES IN THE VESTRY – of the success of which we have no doubt – unless we had good reason to suppose that John Murray can command a public denied to us without diminishing our own public.'

By May of 1956 the matter still had not been settled, though negotiations were proceeding. Betjeman and Davey remained optimistic; though the manuscript had not been sent to typesetters, Betjeman was completing his proofs of the manuscript in hopes of returning it to the SPCK in early June. Still the matter of illustrations was up in the air and there was hope that Piper would return to the project. As of 30 May, Piper was still considering it, writing to Betjeman that 'Mr Davy [sic] sounds so cross that I don't think he'll let me. He . . . seems to resent my not feeling capable of doing Bishops in Motor Cars.' On 4 June, Davey requested that drawings be submitted by the 18th of that month.

Some time within the next two weeks the project collapsed. Murray suddenly announced that the poems were not good enough to merit publication and pulled out of the joint venture. Davey believed the poems were publishable only with illustrations, and concluded that Piper would not do them – at least not in time to ensure the desired Christmas publication. Davey also felt that the poems might be somewhat heavy-handed in their pronouncements of Christian faith and encouraged Betjeman to consider some revision. For his part, Betjeman wisely knew that a radio poem was a unique thing. Preferring perhaps to maintain the integrity of the poems, he wrote to Fr Davey on 19 June that they 'had better give up the project for the time being'.

Around the same time Betjeman wrote to Osbert Lancaster to say that he agreed with Murray 'that the continuation of "Poems in the Porch" is not good enough for publication. . . . They were written only to be spoken on the Western Region at certain seasons in the Church's Year and I never saw them as a book on their own.' This contradicts all that had preceded in his correspondence with the SPCK. Betjeman was hiding his disappointment and frustration, and perhaps a degree of embarrassment as well, by adopting Murray's attitude toward the poems as his own, when clearly he had not felt that way at all. Perhaps he allowed himself to be convinced by Murray. To Lancaster he wrote 'to tell you the truth I think he is quite right' and 'I am inclined to think from my conversation with the Major [Murray] that they are un-illustratable'.

Betjeman's conclusion was that he 'would rather leave them on tape machines'. Alas, those tapes probably no longer exist. The holdings of the BBC's audio archives are limited owing to the custom of erasing recorded programmes in which there were performances of music, and the archives are closed to the public. Moreover, only a few of the broadcast scripts in which the 'Poems in the Porch' appeared survive either, though nearly half are preserved in the BBC's Written Archives Centre at Caversham Park. Some scripts were microfilmed, but most of the paper scripts were destroyed in accordance with standard BBC practice.[12] Fortunately, most – perhaps all – of the poems have survived. The manuscripts of the unpublished poems are preserved in the Betjeman Archive in the McPherson Library at the University of Victoria in British Columbia. Determining the precise number of poems Betjeman read – or the number of times he read poems – is an impossibility. As William Peterson notes concerning Betjeman's broadcasting career at the BBC, 'the documentary evidence is surprisingly difficult to reconstruct'.[13] It is clear, however, that Betjeman read at least 18 'Poems in the Porch' and perhaps as many as 20. A table in the Appendix provides the titles and dates of the broadcasts, and some reliable guesswork concerning the unidentified broadcasts. In this volume I have included, along with the 18 known poems, two poems that Betjeman may have read on air in this series as well as two fragments of poems that, though he left them incomplete, were almost certainly intended to become part of this series.

In the case of many of the heretofore unpublished poems in this volume, there exist several manuscript and typescript versions, some with handwritten alterations that may reflect last-minute, pre-broadcast emendations. My principle in editing these verses has been to present them as they were broadcast – or in a form that most reasonably reflects how the poems were most likely read on air. In some cases, particularly with 'Advent 1955' and 'The Parochial Church Council', significant alterations were made when the poems were eventually published, but it has been my intention to restore these texts to their broadcast states. Where uncertainty remains over particular passages that may or may not have been deleted, I have opted to include those lines, but to encase them in brackets in order to show their doubtfulness. Betjeman did not polish or perfect his drafts, preferring to leave that tedious task to his editors when it came time to publish the poems. For the sake of consistency and clarity throughout the poems, then, I have silently emended Betjeman's spelling, capitalization and punctuation. This has been especially necessary with the unpublished verses, which never benefited from a final edit.

The poems themselves require very little explanation. Written with the specific intention of being read to an audience, they are intentionally direct and straightforward. Betjeman's tones range broadly from satiric and humorous to panegyric and didactic. Although the poems are public utterances, the anxious and personal confession is not uncommon. In such instances, his claims of spiritual assurance are often less convincing than his confessions of uncertainty about the faith. Many of the poems do express doubts. 'And is it true?' he famously asked three times in 'Christmas', reenacting Peter's three denials of Christ. Many more affirm the faith, as in 'Sunday Morning': 'And in a way we can't define / Christ comes to us in Bread and Wine. / I know beyond all trace of doubt / That God is everywhere about.' Betjeman's typical position is somewhere in between, however, as in 'The Conversion of St Paul,' where this generally didactic poem becomes personal at the end: 'But most of us turn slow to see / The figure hanging on a tree / And stumble on and blindly grope / Upheld by intermittent hope.'

Betjeman's subjects typically affirm the elements of faith, celebrate Church history and its calendar, and describe the people of the Church and their places of worship. He recalls the seasons of the church, moving from Advent and Christmas and Epiphany through Shrovetide, Lent, Holy Week and even Harvest Festival. Christmas is the season that most often evokes his muse, comprising four of the poems in this volume. Other church celebrations and holy days comprise five poems, while the rest are devoted to the people and buildings of the Church of England. Of the poems about the people of the Church, Betjeman's wit is at its greatest.

Betjeman is an effective satirist, puncturing the hypocrisy and pomposity of clergy and parishioners alike. He comes down particularly hard on the tendency of parishioners to be fiercely judgmental of others, as in 'Diary of a Church Mouse', 'Blame the Vicar', and 'The

Parochial Church Council'. He can be subtle as well, especially in exposing the foibles of human nature and social customs in such poems as 'Christmas', 'Advent 1955', and 'The Nativity Play'. He also decries the aesthetic desecration of churches in 'Electric Light and Heating', 'Churchyards', 'The Friends of the Cathedral' and 'St Petroc'. Betjeman's satire is almost always genial; most of his outrage is masked by light-hearted rhythms and rhymes, or by the use of rhetorical questions.

Although the ideas and the language are not complex, the poems are nonetheless artistic achievements. His rhymes are always graceful, even when the claims of wit frequently interpose: 'I wish you could meet our delightful archdeacon, / There is not a thing he's unable to speak on' ('Not Necessarily Leeds'). His rhythms can also elicit laughter: 'Talking of messes – you should see / The electrician's artistry, / His Clapham-Junction-like creation / Of pipes and wires and insulation' ('Electric Light and Heating'). Even Betjeman's imagery impresses with its simple and delicate beauty, as when he recalls a visit to rural Ireland during Lent: 'I saw that stream-reflected sky / Above the green weed sliding by, / The sunlight-silvered lichened oak. / I smelt the smell of turf-fire smoke' ('The Lenten Season').

The 'Poems in the Porch' came to an end on 1 February 1957, with Betjeman's reading of 'St Petroc.' With its epic scope on a lyric scale, it provides a fitting conclusion to the series. This poem traces the history of the fictional church of Stoke St Petroc, but uses it as a microcosm for the history of the Church of England. Betjeman begins with the ministry of the eponymous sixth-century Celtic saint and the Norman church built on Saxon foundations. The little nave and chancel would evolve in time with the wealth of the late Middle Ages, before suffering the desecrations of the Reformation and the perhaps even more harmful restorations of a Victorian architect schooled in Gothic revival. Despite the alterations of time and man, however, Betjeman insists that nothing that really matters has changed at all. What Betjeman concludes about this little church suffices as his conclusion about this whole Church as well. It is the endurance of the Church across time, despite the doubt and the hypocrisy, that matters most to him. It is the Church's endurance that he celebrates most in 'Poems in the Porch'.

> The church is there, restored it's true,
> But still the same the ages through,
> With Sacraments and Creed the same
> As in the days when Petroc came.

1 'Christmas Nostalgia', in TRAINS AND BUTTERED TOAST: SELECTED RADIO TALKS, ed. Stephen Games (London: John Murray, 2006), pp. 323–4.

2 Hillier, BETJEMAN: THE BONUS OF LAUGHTER (London: John Murray, 2004), p. 712.

3 Games, OP. CIT., p. 26.

4 'John Betjeman Reads a Selection of His Own Poetry', in Games, OP. CIT., pp. 328–9.

5 'The Faith in the West.' BBC broadcast 6 October 1953. Courtesy of the BBC's Written Archives Centre.

6 'The Faith in the West.' BBC broadcast 10 November 1953. Courtesy of the BBC's Written Archives Centre. The broadcast script shows a last-minute change: the original intention was to call the church 'St Faith's, Low Potter' but was changed during rehearsal to 'Stoke St Petroc'.

7 IBID.

8 'The Faith in the West.' BBC broadcast 8 December 1953. Courtesy of the BBC's Written Archives Centre.

9 John Betjeman, POEMS IN THE PORCH (London: SPCK, 1954).

10 William S. Peterson, JOHN BETJEMAN: A BIBLIOGRAPHY (Oxford: Clarendon Press, 2006), p. 80.

11 Quotations from Betjeman's unpublished correspondence courtesy of the University of Victoria and the estate of Sir John Betjeman.

12 Peterson, OP. CIT., p. 330.

13 Peterson, OP. CIT., p. 329.

Diary of a Church Mouse

Here among long-discarded cassocks,
Damp stools, and half-split-open hassocks,
Here where the Vicar never looks
I nibble through old service books.
Lean and alone I spend my days
Behind this Church of England baize.[1]
I share my dark forgotten room
With two oil-lamps and half a broom.
The cleaner never bothers me,
So here I eat my frugal tea.
My bread is sawdust mixed with straw;
My jam is polish for the floor.

Christmas and Easter may be feasts
For congregations and for priests,
And so may Whitsun.[2] All the same,
They do not fill my meagre frame.

For me the only feast at all
Is Autumn's Harvest Festival,[3]
When I can satisfy my want
With ears of corn around the font.
I climb the eagle's brazen head [4]
To burrow through a loaf of bread.
I scramble up the pulpit stair
And gnaw the marrows[5] hanging there.

It is enjoyable to taste
These items ere they go to waste,
But how annoying when one finds
That other mice with pagan minds
Come into church my food to share
Who have no proper business there.
Two field mice who have no desire
To be baptised invade the choir.

A large and most unfriendly rat
Comes in to see what we are at.
He says he thinks there is no God
And yet he comes . . . it's rather odd.
This year he stole a sheaf of wheat
(It screened our special preacher's seat).
And prosperous mice from fields away
Come in to hear the organ play,
And under cover of its notes
Eat through the altar's sheaf of oats.[6]
A Low Church mouse, who thinks that I
Am too papistical and High,[7]
Yet somehow doesn't think it wrong
To munch through Harvest Evensong,
While I, who starve the whole year through,
Must share my food with rodents who
Except at this time of the year
Not once inside the church appear.

Within the human world I know
Such goings-on could not be so,
For human beings only do
What their religion tells them to.
They read the Bible every day
And always, night and morning, pray,
And just like me, the good church mouse,
Worship each week in God's own house.
But all the same it's strange to me
How very full the church can be
With people I don't see at all
Except at Harvest Festival.

Broadcast 6 October 1953.
Published by the SPCK in 1954.
Published in COLLECTED POEMS in 1958.

1 A coarse woollen curtain.

2 I.e. Pentecost, seven weeks after Easter, commemorating the descent of the Holy Spirit on Jesus' followers. 'Whitsun' alludes to the liturgical colour of white worn on this feast day.

3 A Church of England tradition dating from the mid-nineteenth century, but rooted in pagan customs of celebration for a successful harvest. Churches are decorated with baskets of fruit and other food, which is later distributed among the poor and elderly, and the community gathers in the church for a special service of thanksgiving.

4 A lectern endowed with an eagle carving is a common feature in churches, a symbol often associated with John the Apostle.

5 I.e. autumnal gourds.

6 Betjeman's COLLECTED POEMS erroneously alters the present tense 'Eat' in this line to the past tense 'Ate'. Betjeman's original intention – and the sense of the line – is restored here.

7 References to 'Low' and 'High' Church here and throughout the POEMS IN THE PORCH reflect the division of Anglican churches according to liturgical style, with 'High' churches (to which Betjeman was personally drawn) leaning toward the use of colourful vestments, incense, genuflection and other ritual practices. If 'High Church' generally denotes a church with Anglo-Catholic leanings, a 'Low Church' indicates one more in line with reformed or evangelical theology and worship.

Electric Light and Heating

Alternately the fogs and rains
Fill up the dim November lanes.
The Church's year is nearly done
And waiting Advent not begun.
Our congregations shrink and shrink;
We sneeze so much we cannot think.
We blow our noses through the prayers,
And coughing takes us unawares;
We think of funerals and shrouds.
Our breath comes out in steamy clouds
Because the heating, we are told,
Will not be used UNTIL IT'S COLD.
With aching limbs and throbbing head
We wish we were at home in bed.

Oh! brave November congregation
Accept these lines of commendation;
You are the Church's prop and wall,
You keep it standing for us all!

And now I'll turn to things more bright.
I'll talk about electric light.

Last year when Mr Sidney Groves
Said he'd no longer do the stoves
It gave the chance to Mrs Camps
To say she would not do the lamps,
And that gave everyone the chance
To cry, 'Well, let us have a dance!'
And so we did, we danced and danced
Until our funds were so advanced
That, helped by jumble sales and whist,
We felt that we could now insist
– So healthy was the cash position –
On calling in the electrician.
We called him in, and now, behold,
Our church is overlit and cold.
We have two hundred more to pay
Or go to gaol next Quarter Day.[1]

Despite the most impressive prices
Of our electrical devices,

And though the Bishop blessed the switches
Which now deface two ancient niches,
We do not like the electric light,
It's far too hard and bare and bright.
As for the heat, the bills are hot.
Unluckily the heating's not.

They felled our elms to bring the wire,
They clamped their brackets on the spire
So that the church, one has to own,
Seems to be on the telephone.
Inside, they used our timbered roof,
five centuries old and weather-proof,
For part of their floodlighting scheme,
With surgical basins on each beam.
And if the bulbs in them should fuse
Or burst in fragments on the pews,
The longest ladder we possess
Would not reach up to mend the mess.

Talking of messes – you should see
The electrician's artistry,
His Clapham-Junction-like creation[2]
Of pipes and wires and insulation,
Of meters, boxes, tubes, and all
Upon our ancient painted wall.

If Sidney Groves and Mrs Camps
Had only done the stoves and lamps,
These shameful things we would not see
Which rob our church of mystery.

Broadcast 10 November 1953.
Published by the SPCK in 1954.

1 Quarter Days were the four dates of the year, falling on religious fes-
    tivals roughly three months apart, on which rents and rates were due.
    Though their significance is now limited, certain leasehold payments
    may still be due on traditional quarter days.
2 The busiest railway junction and station in the UK with around 2000
    trains passing through each day.

Christmas

The bells of waiting Advent ring,
    The Tortoise stove[1] is lit again
And lamp-oil light across the night
    Has caught the streaks of winter rain
In many a stained-glass window sheen
From Crimson Lake to Hooker's Green.[2]

The holly in the windy hedge
    And round the manor house the yew
Will soon be stripped to deck the ledge,
    The altar, font and arch and pew,
So that the villagers can say
'The church looks nice' on Christmas day.

Provincial public houses blaze
    And corporation tramcars clang.
On lighted tenements I gaze
    Where paper decorations hang,
And bunting in the red town hall
Says 'Merry Christmas to you all'.

And London shops on Christmas Eve
    Are strung with silver bells and flowers
As hurrying clerks the City leave
    To pigeon-haunted classic towers,
And marbled clouds go scudding by
The many-steepled London sky.

And girls in slacks remember Dad,
    And oafish louts remember Mum,
And sleepless children's hearts are glad,
    And Christmas-morning bells say 'Come!'
Even to shining ones who dwell
Safe in the Dorchester Hotel.[3]

And is it true? And is it true,
    This most tremendous tale of all,
Seen in a stained-glass window's hue,
    A baby in an ox's stall?
The maker of the stars and sea
Become a child on earth for me?

And is it true? For if it is,
    No loving fingers tying strings
Around those tissued fripperies,
    The sweet and silly Christmas things,
Bath salts and inexpensive scent
And hideous tie so kindly meant,

No love that in a family dwells,
    No carolling in frosty air,
Nor all the steeple-shaking bells
    Can with this single truth compare –
That God was man in Palestine
And lives today in bread and wine.

Broadcast on 8 December 1953.
Published in HARPER'S BAZAAR, December 1947.
Published in COLLECTED POEMS in 1958.

1 A slow combustion stove that burned solid fuel. Often installed
  beneath the floor of a church, it heated the nave by convection of
  warm air rising through floor gratings.
2 Betjeman's wordplay has names of artists' colours functioning as
  imaginary places.
3 A leading luxury hotel in London, opened in 1931.

Blame the Vicar

When things go wrong it's rather tame
To find we are ourselves to blame.
It gets the trouble over quicker
To go and blame things on the vicar.
The vicar, after all, is paid
To keep us bright and undismayed.
The vicar is more virtuous too
Than lay folks such as me and you.
He never swears, he never drinks,
He never SHOULD say what he thinks.
His collar is the wrong way round,
And that is why he's simply bound
To be the sort of person who
Has nothing very much to do
But take the blame for what goes wrong
And sing in tune at Evensong.

For what's a vicar really for
Except to cheer us up? What's more,
He shouldn't ever, ever tell
If there is such a place as Hell,
For if there is, it's certain he
Will go to it as well as we.
The vicar should be all pretence
And never, never give offence.
To preach on Sunday is his task
And lend his mower when we ask
And organize our village fêtes
And sing at Christmas with the waits[1]
And in his car to give us lifts
And when we quarrel, heal the rifts.
To keep his family alive
He should industriously strive
In that enormous house he gets,
And he should always pay his debts,
For he has quite six pounds a week,

And when we're rude he should be meek
And always turn the other cheek.
He should be neat and nicely dressed
With polished shoes and trousers pressed,
For we look up to him as higher
Than anyone, except the squire.

Dear people, who have read so far,
I know how really kind you are,
I hope that you are always seeing
Your vicar as a human being,
Making allowances when he
Does things with which you don't agree.
But there are lots of people who
Are not so kind to him as you.
So in conclusion you shall hear
About a parish somewhere near,
Perhaps your own or maybe not,
And of the vicars that it got.

One parson came and people said,
'Alas! Our former vicar's dead!
And this new man is far more "Low"
Than dear old Reverend So-and-so,
And far too earnest in his preaching;
We do not really like his teaching,
He seems to think we're simply fools
Who've never been to Sunday Schools.'
That vicar left, and by and by
A new one came, 'He's much too "High",'
The people said, 'too like a saint,
His incense makes our Mavis faint.'
So now he's left and they're alone
Without a vicar of their own.
The living's been amalgamated
With one next door they've always hated.

Dear readers, from this rhyme take warning,
And if you heard the bell this morning
Your vicar went to pray for you,
A task the prayer book bids him do.
'Highness' or 'Lowness' do not matter,
You are the Church and must not scatter.
Cling to the sacraments and pray
And God be with you every day.

Broadcast on 12 January 1954.
Published by the SPCK in 1954.

1 'Waits' are groups of musicians and singers who walk about the streets
   at night singing Christmas music for gratuities; in essence, carollers.

Septuagesima

Septuagesima – seventy days
To Easter's primrose tide of praise;
The Gesimas[1] – Septua, Sexa, Quinc
Mean Lent is near, which makes you think.
Septuagesima – when we're told
To 'run the race', to 'keep our hold',
Ignore injustice, not give in,
And practise stern self-discipline;
A somewhat unattractive time
Which hardly lends itself to rhyme.

But still it gives the chance to me
To praise our dear old C. of E.
So other Churches please forgive
Lines on the Church in which I live,
The Church of England of my birth,
The kindest Church to me on earth.

There may be those who like things fully
Argued out, and call you 'woolly';
Ignoring creeds and catechism
They say the C. of E.'s 'in schism'.
There may be those who much resent
Priest, liturgy, and sacrament,
Whose worship is what they call 'free';
Well, let them be so, but for me
There's refuge in the C. of E.
And when it comes that I must die
I hope the Vicar's standing by.
I won't care if he's 'Low' or 'High'
For he'll be there to aid my soul
On that dread journey to its goal,
With sacrament and prayer and blessing
After I've done my last confessing.

And at that time may I receive
The grace most firmly to believe,
For if the Christian's faith's untrue
What is the point of me and you?

But this is all anticipating.
Septuagesima – time of waiting,
Running the race or holding fast.
Let's praise the man who goes to light
The church stove on an icy night.
Let's praise that hard-worked he or she,
The treasurer of the P.C.C.[2]
Let's praise the cleaner of the aisles,
The nave and candlesticks and tiles.
Let's praise the organist who tries
To make the choir increase in size,
Or if that simply cannot be,
Just to improve its quality.

Let's praise the ringers in the tower
Who come to ring in cold and shower.
But most of all let's praise the few
Who are seen in their accustomed pew
Throughout the year, whate'er the weather,
That they may worship God together.
These, like a fire of glowing coals,
Strike warmth into each other's souls,
And though they be but two or three
They keep the Church for you and me.

Broadcast 16 February 1954.
Published by the SPCK in 1954.

1 The Sundays preceding Lent. Septuagesima is the third Sunday before
   Lent and commences the pre-Lenten season of Shrovetide.
2 The Parochial Church Council.

Churchyards

Now when the weather starts to clear
How fresh the primrose clumps appear,
Those shining pools of springtime flower
In our churchyard. And on the tower
We see the sharp spring sunlight thrown
On all its sparkling rainwashed stone,
That tower, so built to take the light
Of sun by day and moon by night,
That centuries of weather there
Have mellowed it to twice as fair
As when it first rose new and hard
Above the sports in our churchyard.

For churchyards then, though hallowed ground,
Were not so grim as now they sound,
And horns of ale were handed round
For which churchwardens used to pay
On each especial vestry day.[1]

'Twas thus the village drunk its beer
With its relations buried near,
And that is why we often see
Inns where the alehouse used to be,
Close to the church when prayers were said
And Masses for the village dead.

But in these latter days we've grown
To think that the memorial stone
Is quite enough for soul and clay
Until the Resurrection day.
Perhaps it is. It's not for me
To argue on theology.

But this I know, you're sure to find
Some headstones of the Georgian kind
In each old churchyard near and far,
Just go and see how fine they are.

Notice the lettering of that age
Spaced like a noble title-page,
The parish names cut deep and strong
To hold the shades of evening long,
The quaint and sometimes touching rhymes
By parish poets of the times,
Bellows or reaping hook or spade
To show, perhaps, the dead man's trade,
And cherubs in the corner spaces
With wings and English ploughboy faces.

Engraved on slate or carved in stone
These Georgian headstones hold their own
With craftsmanship of earlier days
Men gave in their Creator's praise.

More homely are they than the white
Italian marbles which were quite
The rage in Good King Edward's reign,[2]
With ugly lettering, hard and plain.

Our churches are our history shown
In wood and glass and iron and stone.
I hate to see in old churchyards
Tombstones stacked round like playing cards
Along the wall which then encloses
A trim new lawn and standard roses,
Bird-baths and objects such as fill a
Garden in some suburban villa.
The Bishop comes; the bird-bath's blessed,
Our churchyard's now 'a garden of rest'.
And so it may be, all the same
Graveyard's a much more honest name.

Oh, why do people waste their breath
Inventing dainty names for death?
On the old tombstones of the past
We do not read 'At peace at last'
But simply 'died' or plain 'departed'.
It's no good being chicken-hearted.
We die; that's that; our flesh decays
Or disappears in other ways.
But since we're Christians, we believe
That we new bodies will receive
To clothe our souls for us to meet
Our Maker at his Judgement Seat.
And this belief's a gift of faith
And, if it's true, no end is death.

Mid-Lent is passed and Easter's near,
The greatest day of all the year,
When Jesus, whom men thought had died,[3]
Rose with his body glorified.
And if you find believing hard,
The primroses in your churchyard
And modern science too will show
That all things change the while they grow,
And we who change in Time will be
Still more changed in Eternity.

Broadcast 6 April 1954.
Published by the SPCK in 1954.

1 A day on which the wardens of the vestry (now more commonly called
  the Parochial Church Council) would host a public assembly for the
  parish.
2 Edward VII, King of Great Britain and Ireland 1901–1910.
3 In response to theological concerns, Betjeman was persuaded in publishing the poem to alter the line to read 'When Jesus, who indeed had
  died.' This text restores the line as he read it on the radio.

The Friends of the Cathedral

At the end of our Cathedral
     Where people buy and sell,
It says 'Friends of the Cathedral',
     And I'm sure they wish it well.

Perhaps they gave the bookstall
     Of modernistic oak,
And the chairs for the assistants
     And the ashtrays for a smoke.

Is it they who range the marigolds
     In pots of art design
About 'The Children's Corner',
     That very sacred shrine?

And do they hang the notices
     Off old crusader's toes?
And paint the cheeks of effigies
     That curious shade of rose?

Those things that look like wireless sets
    Suspended from each column,
Which bellow out the Litany
    Parsonically solemn –

Are these a present from the Friends?
    And if they are, how nice
That aided by their echo
    One can hear the service twice.

The hundred little bits of script
    Each framed in passe-partout[1]
And nailed below the monuments,
    A clerical 'Who's Who'-

Are they as well the work of Friends?
    And do they also choose
The chantry chapel[2] curtains
    In dainty tea-shop blues?

The Friends of the Cathedral –
    Are they friendly with the Dean?[3]
And if they do things on their own
    What does their friendship mean?

Broadcast June 1954.
Published in PUNCH, 14 July 1954.
Published by the SPCK in 1954.
Published in COLLECTED POEMS in 2001.

1 A cheap, adhesive cardboard frame.
2 A small chapel attached to a cathedral, originally established with an
  endowment for a priest to say a perpetual mass for the dead.
3 The head of the chapter of canons in a cathedral church; a cathedral's
  chief priest.

The Bishop

All the village street is humming.
What's the news? The bishop's coming.
All the Mothers' Union say[1]
They'll be baking cakes today.
The bishop will be asked to try
Mrs. Brewer's apple pie.
The bishop will be asked to taste
Mrs. Stewer's almond paste.
The bishop will be given part
Of Mrs. Gurney's cherry tart.
The bishop will, without a question,
Leave with violent indigestion.
In the vicarage the news
Means a raking out of flues
And a polishing of shoes
And a brandishing of brooms
And a turning out of rooms
And a putting on of kettles
And a burnishing of metals.

Such a dusting, such a mending,
You would think the world was ending.
After half an hour of smoking
Which had left the vicar choking,
At last the drawing room fire is burning
And it's time we should be turning
To his wife and daughter seated,
All things ready and completed.
The vicar's little daughter Florence! –
Questions pour from her in torrents
Which her agitated mother
Cannot really check or smother
Save by giving information
Even in this situation.

Thus she waits the bishop's coming,
Nervously her fingers drumming.
And to relieve this strained delaying
I'll record what they are saying,
And to make it clear and neater
Use another style and metre.

'Pray, what is a bishop?' says dear little Floss
To her mother, 'Oh tell me, please do.'
'A bishop, my dear, wears a pectoral cross[2]
And is much more important than you.'

'And pray, why is that?' says this sweet little thing
With her passionate love of research.
'Because,' says her mother, 'he's made by the king
Or the queen, a great lord in the Church.'

'And if you will look at the coin of our realm
Near the name of the monarch it saith
Fid. Def. or F.D., which is Latin, you see,
And means the Defender of Faith.[3]

Our bishops by bishops are always ordained.
They lay hands on their heads. And the track
Of these consecrations, our Church has maintained
To the twelve first apostles goes back.

But remember, dear Florence, that under the skin
They are men (the apostles were too)
With the usual dose of original sin
And the grace to withstand it, like you.'

'And if they are ordinary people, Mamma,
Then can they do just as they like?
Is that why the bishop drives round in a car
While Daddy rides round on a bike?'

'Your father has only to visit the sick
And call on parochial electors,
But the bishop must go in motor-car quick
To admonish recalcitrant rectors.

Then dash up to Parliament, speak in debates
And sit in Church House on committees,[4]
For erecting new churches on building estates
By selling old churches in cities.

There are other things too that a bishop must do
Which seem more important to me,
Such as being the friend and the father in God
To the clergymen here in his see.[5]

In the church of the Celts, which is old, very old,
And brought Christ to the West before Rome
Sent Augustine to Kent, they used, we are told,
To keep all their bishops at home.

And ordaining new priests and confirming the youth
Is really what bishops are for –
To ordain and confirm and, to tell you the truth,
I am sorry they're made to do more.

So soon, when you see our dear bishop processing
In mitre and cope down the lane,[6]
Remember the hand which he raises in blessing
Has also the power to ordain.'

'Oh! thank you very much, Mamma,
How very well informed you are,
I wonder if now you could tell . . .'

(BELL RINGS)

'Thank goodness, Florence, there's the bell.
The bishop's waiting at the door.
So do smooth out your pinafore,
And don't ask questions any more.'

Broadcast 2 November 1954.
Published here for the first time.

1 A worldwide movement of Anglican women, founded in 1876. Through the nurture of the family, the Mothers' Union aims to transform communities worldwide by demonstrating Christian faith in action.

2 A large cross suspended on a chain and worn round the neck in the centre of the chest.

3 FIDEI DEFENSOR, a title given by the Pope Leo X to King Henry VIII in 1521, conferred by Parliament on King Edward VI in 1544, and adopted by all subsequent British monarchs at their coronations. The title has appeared on all British coins since 1714.

4 The headquarters of the Church of England.

5 The jurisdiction of a bishop.

6 As a symbol of his Episcopal office, a bishop wears a mitre, a tall and deeply cleft headdress, as well as a cope, a semi-circular cloak-like vestment.

Advent Bells

The Advent bells proclaim 'Prepare!'
Across the starry winter air
A sweet encirclement of sound
To all the moonlit hamlets round,
'Prepare!' along the whistling hedge
'Prepare!' beyond the parish edge,
Till in the lighted market town
An eight-bell peal begins to drown
The bells of ev'ry neighbouring steeple
'Prepare! Prepare, beloved people!'
'Prepare for whom?' says Mr Flight,
Always grammatically right.
'I think Mahomet, Moses, Buddha
Were just as good as Christ – and good-er.
Oh, yes,' he says, 'Christ was a teacher,
A charming man and splendid preacher.
But do you also think him God?
Dear me,' he says, 'how very odd.

I fear I can't be troubled with
So highly primitive a myth.'
But still the bells ring out the news
Quite unaffected by his views.
And every listening Advent brings
Its message down on angels' wings
That He who made the stars and sea,
The universe and you and me,
Took human flesh and lived on earth
And Christmas Eve recalls his birth.
And men who know the truth's profound
Have collars on the wrong way round,
And for most miserable pay
Give up their lives to teach His way.
What is His way? The bells ring out,
'Come you to church and worship Him
Upon your knees if faith is dim.'

And is He God? Yes. We believe Him
When we in bread and wine receive Him
In very childlike humble faith
Prepared for life, prepared for death
By sacrament and prayer and praise.

I'll tell a tale to you to prove
The way in which God works by love.
I'll call the man Emmanuel Seed –
He did not hold with any creed,
He never went to church on Sunday,
His Sunday was the same as Monday
Except that he could read of crime
And lie in bed till dinner time.
He was a decent friendly type
Who liked his pint and liked his pipe.

Emmanuel's vicar was a man
Of guile. He had a clever plan.
He said to him, 'Emmanuel,
That you're a joiner I know well.[1]
I wonder now if you would jib
At helping me construct a crib?
I want a model of a stable,
And make it quickly as you're able
To be in Church by Christmas day
For when the children come to pray.'
Emmanuel thought, 'Well, that is funny:
He isn't asking me for money,
He asks me just to use my hands.
If that is all that he demands,
I'll have a try. I'll thatch it too.
I'll show him just what I can do,
And then he'll know the likes of we
Who don't believe are good as he.'

He made it. 'My! you've done it well,
We're mighty pleased, Emmanuel,'
Said Harry Hawke, the people's warden.[2]
'It's better than our Easter garden.[3]
Why don't you come and see it lit
With all the figures put in it?'
Emmanuel said he wouldn't mind,
He'd come if so he felt inclined.
He came not once, but twice or thrice.
He thought church services were nice,
And soon he thought them more than that.
'Now what's the vicar getting at?'
'I know that I have been baptised,
I'm darned if I'll be catechised
Like any kid.' But, truth to tell,
The bishop confirmed Emmanuel.

Emmanuel's still a pleasant type
Who likes his pint and likes his pipe

But now our friend Emmanuel Seed
Is buttressed by the Christian creed
And still the friend of all in need.

This tale is only told to prove
A way in which God works by love.
Seed built a stable for the Lord –
The Christian faith was his reward.

Broadcast 14 December 1954.
Published here for the first time.
Title supplied.

1 An ornamental wood worker.
2 As distinct from the rector's warden, who is appointed by the priest-in-charge of a parish, the people's warden is elected to the vestry leadership by the congregation of a parish.
3 A miniature display of flowers and Easter symbols (ranging from a cross or tomb to eggs and hot-cross buns) and sometimes human figures. Often made by school children, it is used to retell the Easter story.

The Conversion of St Paul

Now is the time when we recall
The sharp conversion of St Paul.
Converted! Turned the wrong way round –
A man who seemed till then quite sound,
Keen on religion – very keen;
No one, it seems, had ever been
So keen on persecuting those
Who said that Christ was God and chose
To die for this absurd belief
As Christ had died beside the thief.
Then in a sudden blinding light
Saul knew that Christ was God all right[1]
And very promptly lost his sight.
Poor Paul! They led him by the hand,
He who had been so high and grand,
A helpless blunderer, fasting, waiting,
Three days inside himself debating
In physical blindness: 'As it's true
That Christ is God and died for you,
Remember all the things you did
To keep His gospel message hid.

Remember how you helped them even
To throw the stones that murdered Stephen.
And do you think that you are strong
Enough to own that you were wrong?'
They must have been an awful time,
Those three long days repenting crime,
Till Ananias came and Paul[2]
Received his sight and more than all
His former strength and was baptised.

Saint Paul is often criticised
By modern people who're annoyed
At his conversion, saying Freud
Explains it all. But they omit
The really vital point of it,
Which isn't HOW it was achieved
But what it was that Paul believed.
He knew as certainly as we
Know you are you and I am me
That Christ was all He claimed to be.

What is conversion? Turning round
From chaos to a love profound.
And chaos too is an abyss
In which the only life is this.
Such a belief is quite all right
If you are sure like Mrs Knight[3]
And think morality will do
For all the ills we're subject to.
But raise your eyes and see with Paul
An explanation of it all.
Injustice, cancer's cruel pain,
All suffering that seems in vain,
The vastness of the universe,
Creatures like centipedes and worse,
All part of an enormous plan
Which mortal eyes can never scan
So out of it came God to man.

Jesus is God and came to show
The world we live in here below
Is just an antechamber where
We for His Father's house prepare.

What is conversion? Not at all
For me the experience of St Paul,
No blinding light, a fitful glow
Is all the light of faith I know
Which sometimes goes completely out
And leaves me plunging round in doubt
Until I will myself to go
And worship in God's house below –
My parish church – and even there
I find distractions everywhere.

What is conversion? Turning round
To gaze upon a love profound.

For some of us see Jesus plain
And never once look back again,
And some of us have seen and known
And turned and gone away alone,
But most of us turn slow to see
The figure hanging on a tree
And stumble on and blindly grope
Upheld by intermittent hope.
God grant before we die we all
May see the light as did St Paul.

Broadcast 25 January 1955.
Published in THE LISTENER, 10 February 1955.
Published in UNCOLLECTED POEMS in 1982 and in
COLLECTED POEMS in 2001.

1 When it was first published in THE LISTENER, two weeks after the broadcast, the poem used Paul's original name, Saul, in this one place, and manuscript drafts also reveal Betjeman using the name 'Saul' in this line. Presumably, then, he used 'Saul' here when he read the poem on the radio. When the poem was finally published in a collection of Betjeman's in 1982, the name was altered to 'Paul'. This edition restores Betjeman's original intention. Late drafts of the poem, such as the copy in Betjeman's hand in the British Library (Add. MS 71935, ff. 175–6), reveal additional lines that were excluded from the broadcast version of the poem at the last minute.

2 Acts 9 reports that Ananias was sent by God to heal Paul's blindness and to bring him into the ministry of the Church.

3 Margaret Knight had attacked Christianity on BBC radio in January 1955.

The Lenten Season

Now when the Lenten season comes
I think it's like the roll of drums,
A warning to the band to play
With all its brass on Easter day.
Mid-Lent is past – Refreshment Sunday – [1]
Followed by un-Refreshment Monday.
Eighteen more days of solemn warning
Before the Resurrection morning.
I wonder which is more surprising –
The Birth of Christ or His arising?
I wonder which indeed is stranger –
God being a Baby in a manger
Or God with body glorified,
Walking and talking when He'd died?
The facts indeed are strange enough
And doubters tell you 'folklore stuff'
Yet doubting Thomas did demand
To see the nailprints in each hand,
To see the wounds in Jesus' side,
And saw them and was satisfied.

'Lord, I believe.' First joy! then grief.
'Forgive, Oh Lord, my unbelief.'
And for myself, I find that doubt
Assails me often. But without
The certainty that Christ was God
This world would seem to me most odd.
I'd hate to think that I exist
Because some nuclear physicist
Has not, as yet, blown up the earth
And done away with life and birth.
I'd hate to think our final fate
Was at the mercy of the State,
That love and joy and all ambitions
Were made for us by politicians.
There must, there must be something more.
Roll back the stone! The tomb explore.

This time last week I was away
In Ireland on a holiday,
And all that week I heard no news
Of H-bombs, China, Arabs, Jews,
But heard instead the jingle-jog
Of ass-carts trotting to the bog
And watched the morning mist that fills
The space between the dark blue hills
Dissolve, as sunlight filtered through
To show a sky of paler blue.
I saw that stream-reflected sky
Above the green weed sliding by,
The sunlight-silvered lichened oak.
I smelt the smell of turf-fire smoke.
I saw the willows burning red
With life-sap waiting to be shed
In rabbit-furry buds of palm,

And in this great awaiting calm
Christ's Resurrection really seemed
Not just a wish-fulfillment dreamed
By theologians but a fact
Like any God-directed act
As certain as the rising power
Which makes the bud burst into flower.
So now in Lent's last fortnight comes
A quickening in that roll of drums,
That warning to the band to play
With all its brass on Easter Day.

Broadcast 22 March 1955.
Published here for the first time.
Title supplied.

1 The fourth Sunday in Lent, also known as Mothering Sunday, referring
  to the authorized relaxation or breaking of one's Lenten fast on this
  day.

The Parochial Church Council

Last week a friend remarked to me,
'Now, should I join our P.C.C.?'
I answered rather priggishly,
'You're a communicant. You can
And want to help your clergyman.
Parochial church councils are
From parish councils different far'
I said, 'And district councils too
Have very different things to do,
For district councils raise the rates
And have political debates.
If one side says "Preserve the town",
The other side says "Pull it down!"
And parish councils try to make
The district council keep awake
To local practical affairs –
Like village bus-shelter repairs.

From parish to parliament and queen,
A mighty structure thus is seen –
Endless committees in between.
And I suppose that it occurred
To someone as not quite absurd
To make our Church of England be
A similar democracy.
The Church Assembly's near the top,[1]
Where people talk until they drop;
Next come diocesan committees,
Like mayors and aldermen in cities.
The equivalent to R.D.C.s
Are ruri-decanal jamborees,[2]
And at the bottom of the tree
We find the homely P.C.C.

For P.C.C.s were really made
To give your local vicar aid,
And I have always understood
That most of them are very good –
Where lay folk do what jobs they can
To help their church and clergyman.
But in small villages I've known
Of ones which make the vicar groan
And wish he could be left alone.
So just you come along with me
To a really dreadful P.C.C.'
'Tis evening in the village school,
And wedged into an infant's stool
A large parishioner is sitting
Glancing at us above her knitting.

The farmers sit (they make one laugh)
In desks too small for them by half.
Prim ladies brooding for a storm
Are ranged like infants, on a form.[3]
We read the text that hangs above
In coloured letters, 'GOD IS LOVE'.
The vicar takes the teacher's chair,
A dreadful tenseness fills the air.
'We will begin,' he says, 'with prayer.'
We do. It doesn't make things better.
The vicar reads the bishop's letter –
Diocesan this and quota that –
He might be talking through his hat;
This is not what they've come about.
But now the devil's jumping out
For now we have the church accounts,
And as they're read, the tension mounts.

This vicar has been forced to be
The treasurer of this P.C.C.
As no one else will volunteer
To do the hard work needed here.
'Well, Vicar, do I understand
Last year we had six pounds in hand'
Says Farmer Pinch who's rich and round
And lord of ninety thousand pound,
'And this year you are three pound ten
In debt – and in the red again?
Now, Vicar, that is not the way
To make this parson business pay.
You're losing cash. It's got to stop
Or you will have to shut up shop.'

The tactless vicar answers, 'Sir,
Upon the church you cast a slur.
Church is not trade.' 'Then time it were,'
Growls Farmer Pinch. And now Miss Right
Who has been spoiling for a fight –
Miss Right who thinks she's very Low
And cannot bring herself to go
To services where people kneel,
Miss Right who always makes you feel
You're in the wrong, and sulks at home
And says the vicar's paid by Rome –
Cries, 'If the vicar and his pals
Spent less on popish fal-de-lals
Like altar candles and such frills
Perhaps we then could pay our bills.'
The fight grows furious and thicker,
And what was meant to help the vicar –
This democratic P.C.C. –
Seems just the opposite to me.

The meeting becomes charged with hate,
And turns the devil's advocate.
Its members never go to church.
Admittedly you'd have to search
A lot of villages to find
A P.C.C. that's so unkind,
But everywhere, just now and then,
The devil gets at groups of men.
So if you join your P.C.C.
Be calm and full of charity.

Broadcast 19 April 1955.
Published in UNCOLLECTED POEMS in 1982 and in COLLECTED
POEMS in 2001.

1 Renamed in 1970 the General Synod.
2 Rural decanal conferences were gatherings of lay representatives of
parishes located in rural deaneries. Betjeman makes this R.D.C. the
ecclesiastical equivalent of the rural district council, a governmental
administrative unit.
3 I.e. like children perched on backless school benches.

Sunday Morning

The Reverend Martin Willson wrote[1]
To me a most disturbing note
Demanding of me Christian views
On current matters in the news
To be done in verse, and I refuse.
But let me now go on to say
I'll try it in another way
From what this Godly man intended
And hope he will not be offended,
For politicians bore me stiff.
I do not care the least bit if
Turkey and Persia make a pact,
Or Herbert Morrison is sacked.[2]
The news for me has lost its sting.
It is an artificial thing
Invented by the papers to
Alarm such folk as me and you.

If you don't think so, stay awhile
On some remote Atlantic isle
Without a newspaper and see
How happy you will come to be.
When you return to England's shore
You'll find things as they were before.
But there's a far, far simpler way
Than mere escape. But that's to pray
And go to church. Oh dear, oh dear,
I sound an awful prig, I fear.
But let me show you what I mean,
Please visualise a country scene –
It's Sunday morning, there's the bell
For early service. You can tell
That it is Sunday everywhere,
For Sunday calm is in the air.

Even the dog forgets to bark,
Cattle are silent in the park,
The poultry scratch with Sunday peace
And now before the bell notes cease
I rise reluctantly from bed.
For one more doze? No, church instead.
The tinkle tinkle, loud and plain,
Hurries me up the well-known lane,
And there's the church and here's the door,
The sun shines on the old stone floor.
Only a few are kneeling round,
The country silence is profound.
And when the well-known words are said
Over our offering, wine and bread,
And in a way we can't define
Christ comes to us in bread and wine,

I know beyond all trace of doubt
That God is everywhere about.
Intensely here with us is He
Who made the stars and land and sea.
My calm walk home is one thanksgiving
First for the glorious gift of living,
Then gratitude that I can see
The graceful beauty of a tree,
And joy my homeward walk attends
For love of family and friends.
The intricate beauty of a fly,
The awe-inspiring depth of sky,
From small to great I only scan
One part of an enormous plan,
Delicate, timeless, without end,
Too much for me to comprehend.

But in this Sunday morning mood
I know that God is great and good,
Great in the depth of sky and sea,
Good in becoming Christ for me.
The breakfast waits, the bacon cools,
And here's the paper: football pools,
Riots in Cyprus, trouble in Greece,
Russia, it seems, is keen on peace.
A Christian comment on the news?
Dear Martin Willson, I refuse.

Broadcast 7 October 1955.
Published here for the first time.
Title supplied.

1 Head of religious programming for BBC West of England Home
  Service.
2 Labour politician and heir apparent to Clement Atlee since the 1930s
  (1888–1965).

Advent 1955

Cold December breezes stir
With sea-like sounds our lone Scotch fir.
It's dark at breakfast, dark at tea,
And in between we only see
Clouds hurrying across the sky
And rain-wet roads the wind blows dry
And branches bending to the gale
Against great skies all silver-pale.
The world seems travelling to a place,
And travelling at a faster pace
Than in the leisured summer weather
When we and it sit out together,
For now we feel the world spin round
On some momentous journey bound.
Journey to what? to whom? to where?
The Advent bells call out 'Prepare,
Your world is journeying to the birth
Of God made Man for us on earth.'

And how, in fact, do we prepare
For the great day that waits us there –
The twenty-fifth day of December,
The birth of Christ? For some it means
An interchange of hunting scenes
On coloured cards. And I remember
Last year I sent out twenty yards,
Laid end to end, of Christmas cards
To people that I scarcely know –
But who'd sent one to me, and so
I had to send one back. Oh dear!
Is this a form of Christmas cheer?
Or is it, which is less surprising,
My pride gone in for advertising?
The only cards that really count
Are that extremely small amount
From real friends who keep in touch
And are not rich but love us much.

Some ways indeed are very odd
By which we hail the birth of God.

We raise the price of things in shops,
We give plain boxes fancy tops,
And lines which traders cannot sell
Thus parcelled go extremely well.
We dole out bribes we call a present
To those to whom we must be pleasant
For business reasons. Our defence is
These bribes are charged against expenses
And bring relief in income tax.
Enough of these unworthy cracks!
'The time draws near the birth of Christ',
A present that cannot be priced,
Given two thousand years ago.
Yet if God had not given so
He still would be a distant stranger
And not the baby in the manger.

Broadcast 2 December 1955.
Published in UNCOLLECTED POEMS in 1982 and in
COLLECTED POEMS in 2001.

The Nativity Play

Before the Christmas holiday
We acted our Nativity play.
The bells rang out, the stars were bright,
The church was lit by candlelight.
That evening there were darkened panes
In lonely farms down moonlit lanes,
For almost everyone was led
To see the Babe and stable shed.
We came by bike and car and cart
And some had children taking part
And some were acting in it too
And some had backstage work to do
Like helping little ones to dress,
So that the church I must confess
Was full – up to the very door,
Fuller than ever known before.
The baby was a real one lent
By Mr and Mrs William Kent.

When it began to whine and wriggle
I fear it made the shepherds giggle.
I heard the Vicar's wife say clear
In tones which everyone could hear,
'We'll have a doll another year,'
And this remark gave grave offence
As we expected to the Kents.
A member of the heavenly choir
Had insecurely fixed the wire
Which to her shoulders clipped her wings
And so, of course, she lost the things.
But still, in spite of little hitches
And lots of deft, last-minute stitches,
The play went smoothly on the night
And was a deeply moving sight.
I heard one disapprover say,
'I came to scoff but stayed to pray.'

Oh, when that final scene takes place
Within the crowded stable space
With shepherds sitting on the floor
And Joseph by the stable door,
The mother Mary with her child
Looking so good and sweet and mild,
We all forget her part is played
By a noisy, buxom village maid
Whom we all know, because the play
Takes us two thousand years away
When God came to the Holy Land,
The universe in His small hand.
The world's creator a baby boy,
No wonder we sing songs of joy.

Then comes one of the strangest things:
The entry of three Eastern kings,
Three wise men who have traveled far
Led on to Jesus by a star
As we were led by bells and light
To come to see the play tonight.
How did they know the Child was more
Than just a baby to adore,
But God Himself? How did they know?
Yet it undoubtedly was so.
Three rich and clever men brought presents
To this poor stable full of peasants
And laid them at a baby's feet.
Could there be worship more complete?

For me these three kings symbolise
Jesus revealed to Gentile eyes.
Not just to Jews was Christ revealed
Nor from the rest of us concealed.
He was hailed as God by learned men
From far away. Today, when
I hear of clever scientists
Becoming sure that God exists
And think the Christmas story true,
And when I hear of highbrows who
After long thought at last decide
That Christ was God, the Church His Bride,
I thank Him for those star-led three
Remembered at Epiphany.

Broadcast 6 January 1956.
Published here for the first time.
Title supplied.

Three Crosses

Three crosses stand upon a hill
So black against the sky and still,
So still and black against the sky –
And as I gaze I wonder why
THREE crosses stand, the middle one
Bearing the body of God's son
While robbers either side of Him
Hang dull and criminal and grim.
You'd think it most undignified
To die with thieves on either side,
Not right that God, the King of Kings
Should be mixed up with crime and things,
Most unrespectable to die
In such unsavoury company.
Well, hang respectability,
Was ever such humility?
Those crosses either side of God
Are natural and right, not odd,
And if I may I'll try to show
Just why it is I think them so.

When in Gethsemane Jesus prayed
I wonder was He not afraid?
'If it be possible,' He said,
'Remove this cup from me,' and dread
Of all indignities in store,
The scourging and mocking that He bore,
The carrying of the Cross, the blows,
All these within His mind arose,
For Jesus, don't forget, was Man
With flesh like ours, and so He can
Know what it is to feel the pain
Of being betrayed and whipped and slain.

Have you had friends you trusted who
Have let you down? Well, Jesus too
Had friends, a dozen, one of whom
Stealthily left that Upper Room
And sold his master to His doom.

And when the time of trial drew near
His other friends ran off in fear.
Have you known what it is to be
Liked and respected? So did He.
And then known what it is to fall
Into contempt? Christ knows it all.
Have you done what you didn't ought
And then unluckily been caught
And sent to gaol, not merely fined?
Well, keep this healing thought in mind,
Jesus did nothing wrong, but He
Was stripped and nailed upon a tree.

I well can understand that thief
Who gave his agony relief
By calling from his cross, 'Art thou
The Christ? Well save the three of us now,'
While disbelieving in his heart.

I must confess that for my part
In time of pain and mortal stress
I've been like him, my trust grown less
And thought that Christ can never know
The suffering I undergo.
Oh, when my life draws near its end,
God give me grace to make amend
For wrongs I've done. Give firm belief,
May I be like the penitent thief
And turn to Christ with trusting eyes
And hear Him promise Paradise.

Three crosses stand upon a hill
So black against the sky and still,
So still and black against the sky
The three of them. And we stand by.

After the pain, the blest relief,
After the doubt, the firm belief,
After the dark, the dread, the sinister,
The moment comes when angels minister.
The sap is rising in the trees
A scent of spring is in the breeze.
Good Friday passes. After gloom
Christ bursts in glory from the tomb.

Broadcast 30 March 1956.
Published here for the first time.
Title supplied.

Honest Doubt [1]

Great brutes there are whom no afflictions touch
    While good men often die in dreadful pain.
Why must I call God 'good' and love him much
    If he won't make this strange conundrum plain?

It seems a most unlikely thing to me
    That one poor Jew two thousand years ago
Was God who made the stars and earth and sea.
    What reasons have you for supposing so?

Broadcast 12 October 1956.
Published in ORBIS, Autumn 1983.

1 Betjeman's friend, the Rev Gerard Irvine, composed responding
  quatrains to answer Betjeman's doubts, and they read their verses
  together on air that evening. Martin Willson did not encourage a
  repeat performance. Irvine's verses have not, apparently, survived.

St Petroc[1]

Well yes, perhaps I am a ghost
With longer memory than most
And used our Western land to know
Just fifteen hundred years ago
And saw the corachs with their sails[2]
Carrying Celtic Saints from Wales,
Among them Petroc, he who came
And gave this place its Christian name.
St Petroc, praise of God, his theme,
Waist deep in our brown Moorland stream.
St Petroc with his staff and bell
And draughty, stone-built beehive cell,
St Petroc at his holy well
Baptising heathen, years before
Augustine reached the Kentish shore.
If Petroc's time you would recall,
Look in our ferny churchyard wall
And you will see, all black with moss,
The stone shaft of a Celtic cross.

Stoke is a Saxon name for place
The prefix of that conquering race
Whose treatment of the Celts was shabby.
Years later when a Norman abbey
Built on St Petroc's sure foundation
Its little outpost mission station,
St Petroc's name was kept to show
Which Stoke we were, so strangers know
Stoke Petroc from Stoke Gabriel,
Stoke Climsland and Stoke Damarel.
And in my role of ghost I see
The Norman church there used to be
Nine hundred years ago. 'Twas small,
Just nave and chancel, that was all.
The high-up slatted windows might
In summer weather dimly light
The font we still have got, the floor,
The painted walls and rounded door,
The chancel arch with carved respond,
The altar richly dark beyond.

Three centuries pass, and now I view
Our Stoke St Petroc builded new.
A family chapel on the east
Was added, with its chantry priest,
A new south aisle, a gilded screen.
With painted saints in red and green.
[The granite font and thick north wall
Above the Norman kings recall.][3]
The church was spacious, filled with light
From stained-glass windows, silver bright,
Showing in style you now called 'quaint'
The legend of the local saint.
Christ's passion in the glass is told,
His mother shone in blue and gold.
The roof was like an upturned boat,
And in its ribs carved angels float.
Here in the nave some kneel to pray
While others talk and children play,
For Stoke St Petroc Church is all
The poor folk have – their village hall,

Their club and school; the parish heart
Is this used nave, the people's part.
But there beyond the carven screen
The twinkling altar lights are seen
[Profaner feet have never trod,
This is the place for priests of God].
To keep these altars richly dressed
Merchants and guilds have given their best
And paid a chantry priest to say
Mass for their families every day.[4]

Three centuries have worn the stone
And George the Third is on the throne.
The screen is there, but where the rood
Above the painted panels stood
With Christ on cross, the royal arms
Displays its handsome, sculptured charms.

[The Reformation's been and gone
And what we've left to look upon
Is still like what was there before,
A good deal less, a good deal more.]
The chantry chapel's furnished new
To make a curtained family pew.
Communion's in the English tongue
And metric'lly the Psalms are sung
From the west gallery by a choir.
The pulpit is a good deal higher
And tall box-pews hide sleeping heads.
The old stained glass has lost its leads[5]
And clear glass has been substituted.

The parson locally reputed
To be a man of mighty learning
Does little for the sum he's earning;
He preaches only once a week
With long quotations from the Greek
With which no villager can grapple
So most of them have gone to Chapel.[6]

In 1881 the squire
Decided that he ought to hire
The smartest London architect
For Stoke St Petroc to inspect
Our church. And when the great man came
And left, things weren't at all the same.
He said the screen was 'far too late
For a church of such an early date',
And so alas! he cut it down.

He sold the pews for half-a-crown
And tiled the floors just like a sink
And glazed the windows green and pink.
He scraped the plaster off the walls
And put in pitch-pine pews and stalls.
The changes were indeed immense
And so, of course, was the expense.

And now it's 1957,
And still we try to get to heaven.
The church is there, restored it's true,
But still the same the ages through,
With sacraments and creed the same
As in the days when Petroc came.

Broadcast 1 February 1957.
Published here for the first time.
Title supplied.

1 Celtic saint who ministered in southwestern England in the sixth century. He founded a monastery near Padstow, a region nearly sacred to Betjeman.

2 A coracle; a small wickerwork boat covered in hides.

3 Bracketed passages are found in the typescript of this poem in the University of Victoria, McPherson Library Special Collections, Betjeman Archive, PUF 111. It is uncertain whether these lines were included in the actual radio broadcast.

4 See 'The Friends of the Cathedral,' fn. 2.

5 The frames of the panes in a stained-glass window are known as 'leads'.

6 At one time, 'chapel' was the Church of England's authorized term for nonconformist Protestant churches, such as Baptist and Methodist churches. The term is still commonly used in Wales.

Not Necessarily Leeds[1]

I wish you could meet our delightful archdeacon,
There is not a thing he's unable to speak on.
And if what he says does not seem to you clear,
You will have to admit he's extremely sincere.

Yes, he is a man with his feet on the ground,
His financial arrangements are clever and sound.
I find as his bishop I'm daily delighted
To think of the livings his skill has united.[2]

Let me take for example St Peter the Least
Which was staffed by a most irresponsible priest.
There are fewer less prejudiced persons than I
But the services there were impossibly High.

Its strange congregation was culled from afar,
And you know how eclectic such worshippers are.
The stipend was small but the site was worth more
Than any old church I have sold here before.

I'm afraid its supporters were apt to forget
The crippling extent of the diocesan debt,
Though our able archdeacon explained to them all
Of his reasons for selling their church and their hall.

I'm a moderate man and averse to extremes
So St George's was hardly the church of my dreams.
It was Classic in style and most needlessly Low
And we felt that, in fairness, it too ought to go.

With the sum the archdeacon obtained for the site
And its very rich living, we now can unite
St George and St Peter and see them again
In a moderate church I've allowed to remain,

A worshipful place which I greatly admire
For the length of its chancel and tone of its choir,
And I've promised to preach them a course during Lent
On How the Diocesan Quota is Spent.

A conjectural reading, possibly broadcast 17 February 1956.
Published in THE SPECTATOR, 1 October 1954.

1 Aroused by the success of coffers-enhancing schemes in the diocese
of London, where the bishop had that year sold St Peter, Great Windmill
Street for £150,000, the Bishop of Ripon and the Archdeacon of Leeds
attempted to close Holy Trinity, Leeds and sell its property. This poem
is inspired by Betjeman's battle with the archdeacon, C O Ellison, in
the pages of THE SPECTATOR that year over the fate of Holy Trinity. In
the end the church was saved.
2 An ecclesiastical income; a benefice.

The St Paul's Appeal [1]

I've turned from Queen Victoria Street
   Down gas-lit lanes on windy nights
To where the wharves and water meet
   And seen the sliding river lights
And looked through Georgian window panes
   At plaster work in City halls
While dominant and distant reigns,
   Queen of the sky, the dome of Paul's.

Young clerks with cheeks of boyish rose
   In bars and cafés underground,
Old clerks who play at dominoes
   Where cigarette smoke hangs around,
Girl secretaries eating beans
   In restaurants with white-tiled walls —
They all know what the City means,
   They all are children of St Paul's.

Directors who with eyes shut fast
    Are driven Esher-wards at three,[2]
And those who leave the City last,
    Gay members of some livery
Looking in vain for cab or bus
    Down cobbled lanes where moonlight falls –
The first and last to leave of us
    Are brooded over by St Paul's.

If in some City church we've knelt
    Shut off from traffic noise and news
And all the past about us felt
    Among the cedar-scented pews,
Or if we think the past is rot,
    Or if our purse has other calls,
Whether we go to church or not,
    Which of us will not help St Paul's?

A conjectural reading, possibly broadcast 7 December 1956.
Published in PUNCH, 27 October 1954, under the title 'Who Will
Help St Paul's?'

1 When the poem was first published in PUNCH, the editors changed the
  title to 'Who Will Help St Paul's?' To reflect Betjeman's intentions, I
  have restored the original title as found in his typescripts and correspondence (British Library Add. MS 71935, ff. 202–5).
2 A typical London suburb, Esher is a town of nearly 10,000 in Surrey,
  near the River Mole.

The Visiting Vicar

In late July when people faint
And blisters form on outdoor paint
And cattle suddenly go mad
And butter suddenly goes bad
Our Vicar likes to go astray
At Eastbourne for his holiday.
And that first Sunday he's away
The church is always rather full
Some people come there to be cool
And others in hope of someone slicker
And better looking than the Vicar
It is a sort of annual bet
What sort of parson we will get
Last summer we had quite a change
The parson was extremely strange
He had th' effrontery to tell
Us there was such a place as hell.

An unfinished manuscript, likely intended to be
broadcast as a 'Poem in the Porch'.
Published here for the first time. Title supplied.

God Bless the Church of England

God bless the Church of England,
The burnt-up lawn which gave
A trodden space for that bazaar
Which underpinned the nave.

And croquet in the twilight
With holidays begun,
The Rector's freckled daughter
And sturdy second son.

The broad herbaceous border,
Which hid the wayward ball
In creeper-clad verandah,
The cool capacious hall.

And it clings [?] in the study*
And pipe-incenséd air
When silent catechumens
Sat round the Rector's chair.

God bless the Church of England
Her comprehensive scope,
The manifold opinions
On what to call the Pope.

Anti-Christ or Primate,
He still looks down and smiles

An unfinished manuscript, likely intended to be
broadcast as a 'Poem in the Porch'.
Published here for the first time.
Title supplied.

* The word 'clings' is conjectured; Betjeman's handwriting is illegible in
  this line.

APPENDIX

Untangling the Sequence of Broadcasts

The history of Betjeman's 'Poems in the Porch' is something of a Gordian knot. Betjeman's own records were exceedingly haphazard; he did not even keep copies of many of the radio poems, entrusting them instead to Martin Willson, director of 'The Faith in the West', the BBC programme in which the 'Poems in the Porch' were broadcast. The BBC's records are a notorious labyrinth. Immeasurable thanks, however, are due to William Peterson, who spent countless hours in the Written Archives Centre at Caversham Park, and through whose monumental bibliography of Betjeman we can begin to make some sense out of the incomplete record of Betjeman's broadcasting career.

Peterson has identified in the WAC some 20 dates on which Betjeman is said to have broadcast a 'Poem in the Porch'. However, for four of those dates no poem is identified. One of these, 30 March 1956, I have been able to identify as the date on which he read 'Three Crosses'. Good Friday fell on that date, and this is the subject of the poem. A number of explanations are possible for the other gaps. One is that Betjeman was scheduled to read and did not, perhaps because he did not have a poem ready at the time. I think this is the case with the unidentified broadcast of 22 February 1955. Peterson identifies six broadcasts between November 1954 and April 1955, but in a 1 June 1955 letter to F N Davey of the SPCK, Betjeman states plainly that he now has 'five new verses' since POEMS IN THE PORCH was published in October 1954. I am inclined to think then that Betjeman was scheduled to read that day but for whatever reason did not.

This leaves two other dates, 17 February 1956 and 7 December 1956, on which Betjeman was scheduled to read a 'Poem in the Porch' but for which no poem has been adequately identified. The same situation may apply here that Betjeman simply did not have a poem ready and cancelled his commitment. On 28 November 1956, Betjeman wrote to the Revd Martin Willson, 'I have been trying like anything to write for you, but I CAN'T do this by December 7th. I really cannot. There is a very gloomy hospital poem I have finished, and that would not be at all suitable. It is all about death.'[1] Peterson suggests that the poem Betjeman had in his mind was 'Before the Anaesthetic', a poem that describes the onset of spiritual doubt just before he undergoes surgery, while church bells ring out in echo of his existential isolation. However, 'Before the Anaesthetic' was first published in 1945, so I do not believe he was actually considering reading this poem on air. The only hospital-themed verse that Betjeman wrote in 1956 was 'Inevitable', a poem inspired by his experiences visiting terminal patients in St Bartholomew's Hospital. Though this poem ends with a benedictory peace, its explorations of the inexorable march of death are indeed gloomy, and Betjeman was correct in anticipating Willson's aversion to the poem for this series.

In the end I remain convinced that he did not read either 'Before the Anaesthetic' or 'Inevitable' in the series of 'Poems in the Porch'.

However, another possibility exists that he may have read a poem that has not yet been identified as a 'Porch' poem. I do not believe that this can be proven; it is nonetheless possible that on those two dates he did read a poem. I have identified two poems by Betjeman, both published in 1954 but never added to the COLLECTED POEMS, that share both subject and tone with many of the known 'Poems in the Porch'. These two poems are 'Not Necessarily Leeds' (published in THE SPECTATOR on 1 October 1954) and 'The St Paul's Appeal' (published in PUNCH on 27 October 1954). We know that Betjeman was willing to read previously or soon to be published poems (including 'Christmas', 'The Friends of the Cathedral', and 'The Conversion of St Paul') when scheduling pressures prevented him from composing original verses. Both 'Not Necessarily Leeds' and 'The St Paul's Appeal' would have made excellent 'Poems in the Porch', and moreover typescripts of these two poems are filed in the British Library's Betjeman collection immediately following typescripts of 'The Friends of the Cathedral'.[2] I include them in this volume with the caveat that I have no real proof that Betjeman read them on the radio but with an open mind to the possibility. However, I separate them in the sequence for the end as their status as 'Poems in the Porch' is purely conjectural. I hypothesize that he would have read 'Not Necessarily Leeds' first (in the February 1956 slot) because of his urgency to stop the destruction of churches, and then read 'The St Paul's Appeal' in the final unidentified slot (December 1956) as its imagery evokes a winter chill.

Peterson has identified 18 complete poems that can be identified as 'Poems in the Porch' (as well as six possible fragments of poems that may have been intended for the programme). Of these 18, it is clear to me that, although no record of the broadcast appears to exist, Betjeman must have read 'The Friends of the Cathedral' in the spring of 1954 – probably in June – as it was published in PUNCH on 14 July 1954; Davey acknowledged receipt of this 'new verse' on 7 July 1954, after Betjeman had already been at work on proofreading the typescripts, but it was included in POEMS IN THE PORCH when that volume was published in the autumn.

Concerning the fragments identified by Peterson as intended for 'Poems in the Porch', one of them ('Till Jesus came') I have identified as a very early draft of 'The Conversion of St Paul'. Two others ('Now the Church's year comes round' and 'Three more weeks to fast and pray') I have examined and found that while they do contain some motifs in common with the 'Poems in the Porch', both also contain very personal elements about his family that makes me think he did not intend them for the radio at all. As for the remaining three, I include one ('In late July when people faint') as an illustration of Betjeman's poetry in process; it is clearly incomplete and unpolished, but it is intriguing to imagine how he might have finished it.[3] For this manuscript I have supplied a title, 'The Visiting Vicar'.

I exclude the other two ('The feast day has come round' and 'For faith and work have shown we will') because they are too fragmentary and illegible to serve as a meaningful representation of the poet's process. Finally, I also include one further manuscript poem not previously identified in Peterson's bibliography, as it has much in common with the other 'Poems in the Porch', and publish it here under the title 'God Bless the Church of England'.[4] It also has the distinct ring of the 'Poems in the Porch', and some of its lines were eventually used by Betjeman in his BBC film, A PASSION FOR CHURCHES (1974).

Despite the gap between the BBC records on the one hand and the printed and manuscript texts on the other, a relatively reliable edition of the 'Poems in the Porch' can be constructed. The following table provides the most accurate listing of broadcast dates and titles that it is currently possible to construct.

1 Qtd. William S. Peterson, JOHN BETJEMAN: A BIBLIOGRAPHY (Oxford: Clarendon, 2006), p. 394.
2 British Library, dd. MS 71935, fols. 194–205.
3 University of Victoria, McPherson Library Special Collections, Betjeman Archive, PUF 054.
4 British Library, Add. MS 71645, fol. 106.

Date	Title	Status
6 October 1953	Diary of a Church Mouse	Known
10 November 1953	Electric Light and Heating	Known
8 December 1953	Christmas	Known
12 January 1954	Blame the Vicar	Known
16 February 1954	Septuagesima	Known
6 April 1954	Churchyards	Known
June 1954	The Friends of the Cathedral	Probable
2 November 1954	The Bishop	Known
14 December 1954	Advent Bells	Known
25 January 1955	The Conversion of St Paul	Known
22 March 1955	The Lenten Season	Known
19 April 1955	The Parochial Church Council	Known
7 October 1955	Sunday Morning	Known
2 December 1955	Advent 1955	Known
6 January 1956	The Nativity Play	Known
17 February 1956	Not Necessarily Leeds	Conjectural
30 March 1956	Three Crosses	Probable
12 October 1956	Honest Doubt	Known
7 December 1956	The St Paul's Appeal	Conjectural
1 February 1957	St Petroc	Known